EXPLORE THE U.S.A.

VERMONT

Helen Lepp Friesen

LET'S READ
AV2 BY WEIGL™
ADDED VALUE • AUDIO VISUAL

www.av2books.com

LET'S READ AV²
BY WEIGL™
ADDED VALUE • AUDIO VISUAL

Go to **www.av2books.com,** and enter this book's unique code.

BOOK CODE

B 9 6 4 5 5 9

AV² **by Weigl** brings you media enhanced books that support active learning.

AV² provides enriched content that supplements and complements this book. Weigl's AV² books strive to create inspired learning and engage young minds in a total learning experience.

Your AV² Media Enhanced books come alive with...

Audio
Listen to sections of the book read aloud.

Video
Watch informative video clips.

Embedded Weblinks
Gain additional information for research.

Try This!
Complete activities and hands-on experiments.

Key Words
Study vocabulary, and complete a matching word activity.

Quizzes
Test your knowledge.

Slide Show
View images and captions, and prepare a presentation.

...and much, much more!

Published by AV² by Weigl
350 5th Avenue, 59th Floor
New York, NY 10118
Website: www.av2books.com   www.weigl.com

Library of Congress Cataloging-in-Publication Data
Friesen, Helen Lepp, 1961-
Vermont / by Helen Lepp Friesen.
    p. cm. -- (Explore the U.S.A.)
Includes bibliographical references and index.
ISBN 978-1-61913-411-9 (hard cover : alk. paper)
1. Vermont--Juvenile literature. I. Title.
F49.3.F75 2012
974.3--dc23
                                    2012016584

Printed in the United States of America in North Mankato, Minnesota
1 2 3 4 5 6 7 8 9 16 15 14 13 12

052012
WEP040512

Project Coordinator: Karen Durrie
Art Director: Terry Paulhus

Weigl acknowledges Getty Images as the primary image supplier for this title.

VERMONT

Contents

2   AV² Book Code
4   Nickname
6   Location
8   History
10 Flower and Seal
12 Flag
14 Animal
16 Capital
18 Goods
20 Fun Things to Do
22 Facts
24 Key Words

3

This is Vermont.
It is called the Green Mountain State.
The Green Mountains are in Vermont.

This is the shape of Vermont. It is in the north part of the United States.

Where is Vermont?

N
W E
S

Canada

United States

Pacific Ocean

Atlantic Ocean

Mexico

Three states and Canada border Vermont.

American Indians called
the Abenaki were the first
people to live in Vermont.
They hunted caribou
for food.

The word Abenaki
means "People
of the First Light."

9

The red clover is the state flower of Vermont. It grows wild in fields. Cattle eat red clover.

The Vermont state seal has a cow and four sheaves of wheat.

The seal also has a big pine tree in the middle.

This is the state flag of Vermont. It has pine branches under a crest.

The state motto is near the bottom of the flag.

FREEDOM VERMONT AND UNITY

13

The state animal of Vermont is the Morgan horse. This horse was named after a music teacher.

Morgan horses were used by soldiers in the Civil War.

This is Montpelier. It is the state capital of Vermont. Montpelier was named for a place in France.

Montpelier is one of the smallest state capitals in the United States.

Maple syrup is made in Vermont.
It is made with sap from maple trees.
More than 1 million gallons of syrup
are made in Vermont each year.

A maple tree must be
at least 40 years old
to be tapped for sap.

Vermont is known for its beautiful hills and trees.

People come from around the world to see the colorful leaves in the fall.

VERMONT FACTS

These pages provide detailed information that expands on the interesting facts found in the book. These pages are intended to be used by adults as a learning support to help young readers round out their knowledge of each state in the *Explore the U.S.A.* series.

Pages 4–5

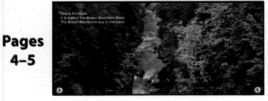

Vermont is one of the smallest states in the United States. It is not heavily populated. Most people in Vermont live in rural areas, small towns, or villages. The Green Mountains are part of the Appalachian Mountains and cover most of the state.

Pages 6–7

On March 4, 1791, Vermont became the 14th state to join the United States. It is one of the New England states, but unlike the others, it is not on the Atlantic Ocean. Quebec, Canada borders Vermont to the north, New York to the west, Massachusetts to the south, and New Hampshire to the east.

Pages 8–9

Iroquois and Algonquin tribes lived in Vermont long before European settlers came. The Abenaki belonged to the Algonquin group. The Abenaki and Iroquois fought to control the region. French explorer Samuel de Champlain arrived in 1609. He helped the Abenaki push back the Iroquois. The French won the battle and declared the land belonged to France.

Pages 10–11

Red clover became the official state flower of Vermont in 1894. Clover improves farmland by adding nitrogen to the soil. The state seal depicts wooded hills with a large pine to represent the Green Mountains. The cow and wheat stand for Vermont farming. The waves at the top and bottom of the seal stand for the sky and the water.

Pages 12–13

The current Vermont flag was adopted in 1923. The Vermont coat of arms is in the middle of a blue background. The Vermont coat of arms is similar to the state seal, with symbols to represent Vermont's industry and scenery. The red scroll at the bottom reads, "Freedom and Unity."

Pages 14–15

In 1961, Governor F. Ray Keyser Jr. named the Morgan horse Vermont's state animal. The first Morgan horse was a small rugged stallion that belonged to music teacher and composer Justin Morgan. This horse was bred to run faster than other horses. The new breed soon became the most common horse in the country.

Pages 16–17

About 7,800 people live in Montpelier. In Montpelier, people can visit the Vermont state house, museums, an art gallery, a nature center, and a farmers' market. The Hubbard Park and Tower is a 194-acre (78-hectare) park with about 7 miles (11 kilometers) of trails for skiing and hiking. The observation tower offers a good view of Montpelier.

Pages 18–19

Vermont is well known for its maple syrup and maple sugar. One maple tree is large enough to yield about 40 gallons (150 liters) of sap. This sap can be used to make 1 gallon (3.7 L) of syrup. There are about 2,000 maple producers in Vermont. Vermont maple products, such as syrup, sugar, and candy, are shipped around the world.

Pages 20–21

More than four million people visit Vermont every year. People come to ski, snowboard, and snowmobile. The fall leaves turn Vermont's hills brilliant colors, with the leaves of the birch, maple, and oak trees turning yellow, gold, orange, and red. People who come to view the fall colors are called "leaf peepers."

KEY WORDS

Research has shown that as much as 65 percent of all written material published in English is made up of 300 words. These 300 words cannot be taught using pictures or learned by sounding them out. They must be recognized by sight. This book contains 60 common sight words to help young readers improve their reading fluency and comprehension. This book also teaches young readers several important content words, such as proper nouns. These words are paired with pictures to aid in learning and improve understanding.

Page	Sight Words First Appearance
4	are, in, is, it, state, the, this
7	and, of, part, three, where
8	American, first, food, for, Indians, light, live, means, people, they, to, were, word
11	a, also, big, eat, four, grows, has, tree
12	near, under
15	after, animal, by, named, used, was
16	one, place
19	at, be, each, from, made, more, must, old, than, with, years
20	around, come, its, leaves, see, world

Page	Content Words First Appearance
4	Green Mountains, Vermont
7	Canada, shape, United States
8	Abenaki, caribou
11	cattle, clover, cow, fields, flower, middle, seal, sheaves, wheat
12	bottom, branches, crest, flag, motto, top
15	Civil War, Morgan horse, soldiers, teacher
16	capital, France, Montpelier
19	gallons, sap, syrup
20	fall, hills

MEDIA ENHANCED BOOKS
AV² BY WEIGL™
ADDED VALUE • AUDIO VISUAL

Check out www.av2books.com for activities, videos, audio clips, and more!

1 Go to www.av2books.com.

2 Enter book code.  B 9 6 4 5 5 9

3 Fuel your imagination online!

www.av2books.com